KNOWTH

& Brú na Bóinne

Paul Francis

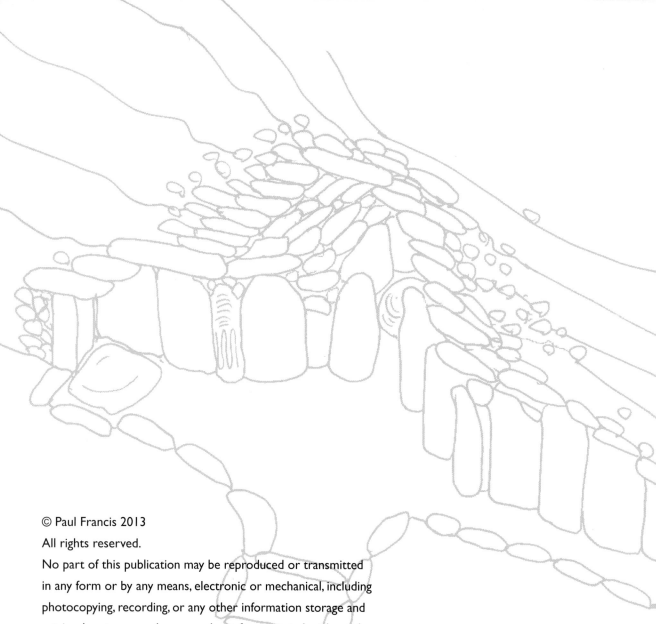

ISBN: 978-0-9926143-0-0

Published by: Charial Publishing

Ireland's Built Heritage series

Designed by: Paul Francis

Editorial Consultant: Tara Horan

Archaeological Consultant: Isabel Bennett

With special thanks to: Clare Tuffy, Aideen Gough and Pat McCusker

All illustrations by the author.

Photos (p 1, 4, 5, 7, 9, 24, 28, 30, 32, 33, 38, 39, 45, 48,) by kind permission of the National Monuments Service, Dept of Arts, Heritage and the Gaeltacht. With thanks to Tony Roche.

Designed and printed in Ireland.

For additional copies e-mail: Paulfrancisdesign@eircom.net

Contents

Knowth revealed

*E*arly archaeologists had always suspected that the giant grass-covered mound at Knowth, close to the River Boyne, was not a natural feature and was related in some way to the, by then, famous Neolithic tomb of Newgrange only 1km away. Fortunately it was not until 1941 that the first excavation of Knowth was undertaken, when the science of archaeology had matured and careful and meticulous methods were employed. R A S Macalister of University College Dublin revealed a kerb of large decorated stones at the base of the mound and thereby established that the large mound at Knowth had indeed been built and was probably as old as Newgrange.

It took an intense public debate, two decades later, over the condition and safety of Newgrange (open since 1699) to draw back the archaeologists and provide the finance for a major excavation in the Boyne Valley. Newgrange was attracting a larger number of visitors with every passing year and was in a dangerous condition. It was decided that Professor Michael J O'Kelly of University College Cork, would carry out a limited excavation, which would clear the way for repair work and for visitor facilities to be installed.

Within sight of Newgrange, excavations had also started at Knowth under the direction of Professor George Eogan of University College Dublin. Intrigued by the questions posed by his earlier excavation of a small passage-tomb at nearby Townleyhall, Prof Eogan opted to seek answers at the larger site of Knowth. The excavations at Knowth and Newgrange were to last much longer than the 'few seasons' anticipated by Prof O'Kelly, as discovery after discovery kept both archaeologists and their teams fully engaged for years to come, in what were to be the largest archaeological excavations ever carried out in Ireland.

During the early years of Prof Eogan's excavation of Knowth, work was concentrated on the northern side, on the ground close to the already exposed kerbstones. These excavations brought immediate and exciting results, unearthing more highly decorated kerbstones and several small passage-tombs. Such was the wealth of discoveries from each layer of archaeology, from the Neolithic to the early 19th century, that a plan was drawn up to methodically examine the entire site using a grid system (visible in the picture above right). Starting in the north, Prof Eogan and his team moved slowly westwards.

In the summer season of 1967, the excavators had uncovered a kerbstone that seemed to indicate that

Professor George Eogan (right) and members of his team at Knowth.

Knowth during the modern excavation and restoration. All the smaller satellite tombs have been excavated and those to the north have been reconstructed. All the kerbstones have been revealed and the eastern passage, on the right of the mound, is undergoing restoration

something lay behind it. Further digging revealed a layer of quartz and granite rolled boulders on the original ground surface, similar to those found at the entrance to Newgrange. Digging further into the mound behind the kerbstone, Prof Eogan and his team first excavated the upper layers belonging to the Early Christian period. Eventually they broke through a layer of loose stoneless soil to a cavity beyond.

The smallest member of the team was sent through to examine the cavity and he excitedly reported that he could see for 20 metres. At first believing it to be the work of the Early Christians, Eogan allowed general excavation work to continue. When a more substantial hole had been cleared, with torch light in hand, it became instantly clear to Prof Eogan from the great carved orthostats that formed the walls,

that he was peering down the passage of a Neolithic tomb. A long crawl, mostly on all fours, sometimes in water, brought them first to a large basin stone discarded in the passage. A carving with large staring eyes and gaping mouth announced the beginnings of the chamber, followed by three sill stones. At last, Prof Eogan and his fellow archaeologists could stand up straight in a chamber built 5,000 years before. Knowth had yielded up one of its greatest secrets to modern people.

There were many more revelations to come in the three decades of excavation that were to follow. Just one year later in 1968, Prof Eogan and his team discovered the eastern chamber and sometime later, the Knowth macehead, two of the greatest discoveries of European Neolithic archaeology.

Brú na Bóinne

About 15km before the River Boyne enters the Irish Sea on the east coast of Ireland, it is forced to turn south by a ridge of high ground. The river slowly returns to its original eastward course in a great curve or bend. The Boyne is joined by another smaller river, the Mattock, which flows into it at about this point. This is Brú na Bóinne or in English, 'the Palace of the Boyne', 780 hectares in area, surrounded and protected on nearly all sides by water.

People living in the Neolithic Age (New Stone Age), over 5,000 years ago, chose Brú na Bóinne to be a place of special religious significance. They built, over many generations, the three great monuments of Knowth, Dowth and Newgrange. Located on the three highest points in Brú na Bóinne, the mounds (tumuli) were meant to be seen from the river and dominate the surrounding landscape. By the time they were completed (3000BC) they were the greatest buildings in the ancient world.

The rituals and festivals associated with the three monuments have long been forgotten, but enough cremated bone and artefacts remained in their chambers for archaeologists excavating in modern times, to define them as tombs, although they had many other purposes such as; as a focal points for the community and as a mark of wealth and territory.

Today Brú na Bóinne is a UNESCO World Heritage Site, protected and managed by the Irish state. At its heart are the three great tombs of Knowth, Dowth and Newgrange, but modern archaeology has discovered many other ritual sites in the landscape of Brú na Bóinne including: over 40 smaller 'satellite' passage-tombs, several henge features, a cursus (thought to be a processional route) and numerous other monuments built in other eras, such as ringforts, monastic settlements and medieval castles.

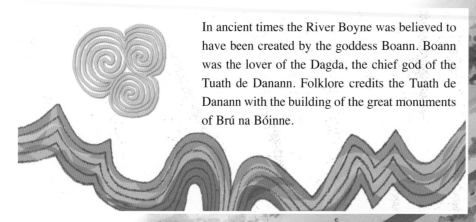

In ancient times the River Boyne was believed to have been created by the goddess Boann. Boann was the lover of the Dagda, the chief god of the Tuath de Danann. Folklore credits the Tuath de Danann with the building of the great monuments of Brú na Bóinne.

River Boyne

Knowth

Irish Sea

Boyne
Estuary

Drogheda

Dowth

River Mattock

Brú na Bóinne

Newgrange

France

Bay of Biscay

Belgium

Germany   Netherlands   Brittanny

● Gavrinis
● Gulf of Morbihan

Denmark   Location of
passage-tombs
in Europe
Stonehenge ●

Wales   **North**
England

North Sea   ● Anglesey

Ireland

● Brú na Bóinne

● Lough Crew

● Carrowkeel
● Carrowmore

Scotland   Atlantic Ocean

● Orkney Islands.

The Atlantic people of the Neolithic age

The Neolithic passage-tombs of Brú na Bóinne are part of a much wider Atlantic tradition of tomb building using megaliths (great stones). From Portugal in the south to Sweden and Denmark in the north, there existed in the Neolithic (New Stone Age 4000BC–2500BC), a passage-tomb building culture, which lasted for thousands of years. While each region had its own style, the similarities amongst these megalithic buildings was much greater than their differences.

The passage-tombs of Spain and Portugal share the greatest similarities in design with the tombs of Brú na Bóinne. Similar artefacts, such as round-bottomed pottery and grave goods from the tombs themselves, are also found in both locations. The passage-tombs of the Gulf of Morbihan in Brittany, France are part of a major centre of megalithic building activity and also share a scale and similarity with those in Brú na Bóinne. The carved art of the interior of one of Brittany's greatest tombs, Gavrinis, bears close comparison with that of Knowth, Dowth and Newgrange.

The European passage-tomb culture of the Neolithic age proves that the people of Atlantic Europe were in regular contact with each other over a prolonged period of time. Ocean-going boats must have travelled the great distances between Spain, France and Ireland (over 1,000km) and eastwards to Denmark and Sweden to trade and swap ideas. Perhaps this was not unusual in Neolithic times, as travel by boat on sea, river and lake was the only efficient way of getting about in Atlantic Europe, a place without horses, the wheel or roads.

In the fourth millennium BC (6,000 years ago), Ireland became a major centre of passage-tomb building. The oldest site is Carrowmore (Co Sligo) and many other passage-tombs were built in the next millennium, such as Loughcrew (Co Meath), Brú na Bóinne and Carrowkeel (Co Sligo). Most of the passage-tombs, of which there are over 170, were built as part of a cemetery, but there are many other lone sites, usually found on high ground and in the northern part of the country.

**Passage-tomb,
Carrowmore, Co Sligo**

Irish passage-tombs

A typical Irish passage-tomb of the Neolithic age (including Knowth, Dowth and Newgrange) contains several common features:

▎ A passage leading to a chamber. The passage can vary greatly in length and height, but can always accommodate a fully grown person

▎ A chamber. The chamber varies in size, shape and height. Recesses are also a common feature, often in a cruciform (cross-shaped) plan

▎ A kerb made of large stones, which defines the shape and size of the passage-tomb

▎ A mound, also know as a tumulus or cairn. It was usually made of small stones, but in larger passage-tombs can be constructed using soil and stone in alternate layers

▎ A basin stone is sometimes found in the chamber or the recesses. They were used as a receptacle for cremated remains and grave goods.

Poulnabrone portal tomb, Co. Clare. These megalithic structures (sometimes known as dolmens) are common throughout Ireland and Europe. They are a type of single-chambered megalithic tomb, usually consisting of three or more upright stones supporting a large flat horizontal capstone.

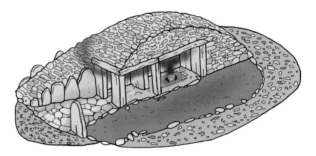

Shanballyedmond court tomb, Co. Tipperary. Court tombs are distinguished by a courtyard situated in front of the entrance which leads to a rectangular chamber. Wedge tombs are another type of megalithic tomb found in Ireland.

Cut-away of a passage-tomb

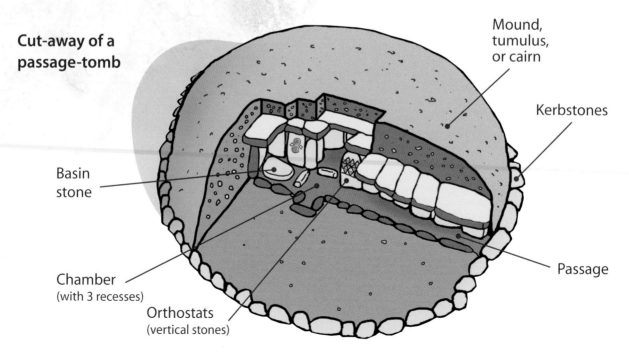

Mound, tumulus, or cairn

Kerbstones

Passage

Basin stone

Chamber
(with 3 recesses)

Orthostats
(vertical stones)

Visitors to the Boyne Valley are often struck by the richness of the farmland stretching out to the horizon in gentle rolling hills. Wheat, barley, cattle, pigs and sheep are farmed here today, much as they were in the stone age, 5,000 years ago. The Boyne Valley was not always productive grassland and farming was not always the way to food production. Six thousand years ago, at the dawn of the New Stone Age, a deep continuous forest covered all of Ireland, punctuated only by mountains and wetlands. A small population (c.3,000) of Mesolithic (Middle Stone Age) people lived on the island as hunter-gatherers.

They hunted wild boar, deer, hare, birds and fish of all sorts. They gathered a diverse range of fruits, plants, berries and shore food from the coast and river valleys where they lived. Mesolithic people moved about, left little trace and hardly changed the land they lived in.

About 6,000 years ago, the most significant change in the way life was lived on the island of Ireland occurred – farming. It is not known whether farming arose independently amongst the Mesolithic people, or if it arrived with new settlers migrating from continental Europe. What is known is that it quickly took hold and became the accepted way of life.

These Neolithic (New Stone Age) people absorbed the existing Mesolithic culture and set about the task of clearing the forest and making the land suitable for farming using a new innovation, the polished stone axe. It was capable of producing large clean cuts and could be used with greater speed and precision in the clearing of woodland. The new farmers changed the landscape

(above) The introduction of the clay pot meant that food could be stored for the winter and for leaner times

(right) The polished stone axe radically altered the Irish Neolithic landscape

(below) Animals found on farms today – goats, cattle, sheep and pigs – began their domestication in the Neolithic era

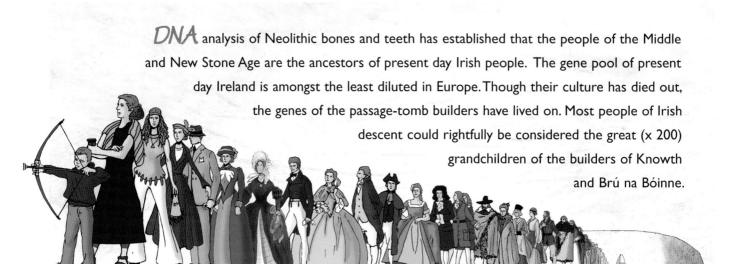

DNA analysis of Neolithic bones and teeth has established that the people of the Middle and New Stone Age are the ancestors of present day Irish people. The gene pool of present day Ireland is amongst the least diluted in Europe. Though their culture has died out, the genes of the passage-tomb builders have lived on. Most people of Irish descent could rightfully be considered the great (x 200) grandchildren of the builders of Knowth and Brú na Bóinne.

slowly but surely, but not all the Mesolithic ways of life were discarded and many of the old ways would still persist.

Time and energy preparing the soil gave Neolithic farmers a sense of ownership of the land and they built large permanent homes made from the materials that they found locally. Split logs were used to create walls for their substantial houses. Straw and rushes created a waterproof thatched roof, a technique which lasted into the 20th century.

The successful production of a food surplus meant that new techniques were employed to store food for future use. Stone querns (below right) were used to grind wheat into flour for bread or the grain could be stored in large pots and used at some future time. Pottery kept hard-won food safe from small creatures and allowed it to be stored for hungrier times, when harvests were poor.

The production of a food surplus allowed people the time to pursue other interests and develop other skills, which didn't necessarily contribute to their day-to-day survival. There was most likely sport, music, art and story telling (perhaps about their own ancestors) in the lives of the people of the Boyne Valley, all of which is now lost and forgotten.

(right)
Neolithic houses could be either rectangular or oval/round. Houses built at the time of Brú na Bóinne were generally of the oval/round type.

Very few Neolithic houses have been found in the Boyne Valley. Entirely made from materials that disintegrate over time, all that remains of a typical Neolithic house would be a hearth, some sherds of pottery and stone tools. Archaeologists look below the original ground level for evidence of post holes. The soil, which has filled these holes over time, is usually a darker colour than the surrounding soil.

Working the land also led to a desire to mark the landscape with structures that would stand out and would be permanent. The people of the Boyne Valley chose to make their greatest, most prestigious and most permanent buildings, the ones associated with their religious beliefs. These buildings would also be the burial place of the people of the community and a place to honour their ancestors.

The 'New Stone Age' was a era defined by the farming revolution and the use of stone as the most important material for tools (there being no metal). There were other important raw materials such as antler, bone, wood, hide and clay which made many everyday things.

Antlers (above) shed from the male red deer were used to make a wide range of implements. The exceptional qualities of elasticity and resistance found in the antler was appreciated by Neolithic people who used them to manufacture implements such as handles for stone knives and drills, ploughs, shovels and pins. The antler pin is amongst the most common artefact found by archaeologists in excavated passage-tombs.

Building Knowth

Building Knowth and the other tombs of Brú na Bóinne must have been a collective and popular decision by the people of the Boyne Valley. They would have been aware from constructing earlier, smaller passage-tombs just what was required and that the proposed great tombs, which were to be built on a scale never seen before, would take decades to complete. Most of their spare time, for the rest of much of their lives, would be given over to building the monuments.

Given the short life span of people, most of those who began the work would not live to see the buildings completed. Pushing them on in this incredible venture was their religious beliefs and a probable belief in an afterlife, which needed to find some expression or mark on the landscape in which they lived, much like the cathedral builders of the Middle ages, 4,000 years later.

We have no way of knowing how the people of the Boyne Valley organised themselves, but the building of Knowth itself would have required an energetic leadership to organise the workforce. A workforce which lived in small family groups scattered throughout the Boyne Valley (and perhaps from other parts of the country) would have needed a rallying call on a daily basis.

Much of the work was probably done in the longer drier days of the summer months, it being the best and safest time to haul and construct. Given the immense challenges posed by construction, the work force may also have gathered in the fallow days of the winter, work perhaps reaching a peak around the time of the winter solstice. Only during the autumn months would work cease when important farming work, such as the harvest, could not be neglected.

The finding and quarrying of hundreds of large stones (most are a sandstone called greywacke) was amongst the first tasks to be carried out. Stone is the defining material of the building and while other materials were used, it was the careful selection of large hard stones which has contributed to the endurance of Knowth over five millennia. The builders set out with the purpose of building a stone monument, one which was required to last forever.

Boats using the inbound tide or the eastward flow of the River Boyne, were probably

Kerbstone 53 is over 3 metres long and 1.5 metres high.

used to transport the 1,600 stones weighing over a tonne (some as heavy as 5 tonnes) used in the construction of the tombs at Knowth. These stones however, still had to be dragged uphill to the site, the highest point in Brú na Bóinne.

Lifting, sledging or using log rollers, or a combination of all three, were the probable methods of moving the stones forward and upwards (the wheel had only just been invented in the Middle-East and was unknown in Europe and the horse was not native to Ireland).

The place name Knowth is an anglicisation of 'Cnogba'. In Irish mythology, Cnogba or Cnoc Bui is the 'home or hill of the goddess Bui, consort of Lugh'.

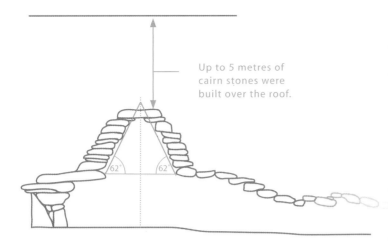

Up to 5 metres of cairn stones were built over the roof.

62° 62°

The eastern chamber roof (left and below) was, at the time of construction, one of the greatest structural projects ever attempted. The dome-shaped roof was built by placing large flat slabs of stone (some are 1.8 metres long) in horizontal layers of ever-decreasing circles, in a style known as corbelling. As each stone was hauled into place, it overhung the one below it, risking the collapse of the entire structure. Only when the final cap stone was in place was the roof secure.

The roof, however, would not only be required to support its own weight, but the massive weight of the cairn which was to be built over and above it.

The construction of the kerb, passages and chambers were probably the first parts of the building to be tackled. Once the first level of vertical stones (orthostats) were placed in secure foundations, smaller stones of about 20cm in diameter were placed around them to further secure and strengthen their position (see right).

For a time the great dome-shaped roof of the eastern chamber would have been free standing. Year after year it would slowly disappear as the cairn was built over and around it

No mortar or concrete was used in the construction of the roof and it has remained intact, waterproof and unaltered for over 5,000 years.

Once the passage and chambers were completed, full attention could be paid to the labour-intensive work of building the cairn. Thousands of tonnes of smaller stones were placed in alternating layers with earth and grass turves. These turves were stripped from the ground around Knowth and proved useful in holding the layer of stone above and below it, in position. With each season of building, the tomb grew higher, more complete and more impressive.

Large orthostats (upright stones) were used to build the passage and chamber. All the weight of the roof is supported by these stones which were chosen for their strength and shape. A part of each orthostat was buried in a trench and back-filled with stones for support

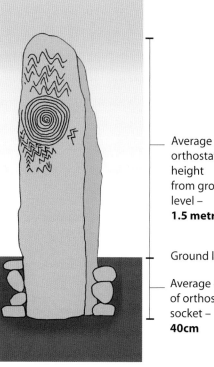

Average orthostat height from ground level – **1.5 metres**

Ground level

Average depth of orthostat socket – **40cm**

Knowth completed

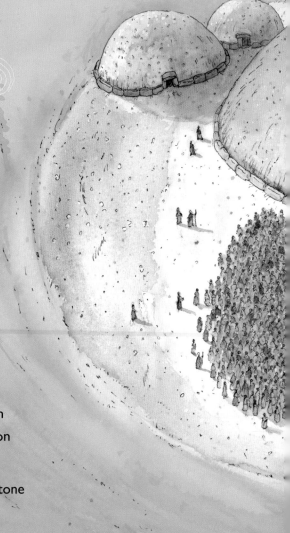

When Knowth was completed, around 5,000 years ago (3000BC), it was the single biggest building in the world. It symbolised the spiritual energy of its builders and most probably was a place of worship and pilgrimage for not only the people of Ireland, but all the Atlantic people of Europe. Viewed from the River Boyne in the Neolithic Age, Knowth, Dowth and Newgrange constituted the greatest complex of buildings in the world.

Knowth would remain the largest building in the world until the construction of the pyramid of Djoser in Egypt in c. 2640BC, a building which fulfilled a similar set of purposes, as a tomb, a monument and as a mark on the landscape. It would be another four thousand years before Knowth would be eclipsed as a building in terms of scale in Ireland by the nearby Cistercian monastery of Mellifont Abbey, built soon after 1142AD.

The exterior appearance of the main mound was probably a finish of stone and earth. The flat level top was probably finished only in stone.

Outside Knowth

The many external features of Knowth, its prominent position on high ground, as well as its great size, indicate that the exterior of the monument was as important to the builders of the Boyne Valley as any other aspect of the building.

Kerbstones

A total of 127 kerbstones, some as long as 3 metres, define the shape of the monument. The entire length of the kerb (285 metres) has all been revealed in recent times, by modern excavations and only three of the original 127 kerbstones are missing, despite the occupation of the site over thousands of years. Most were found upright and in their original positions.

Great attention was taken in the selection and positioning of the kerbstones to attain a regular profile and equalisation of height. The bigger and most regular stones are positioned near the two entrances and many of these are highly decorated. Ninety kerbstones contain at least some decoration and a large proportion of this number are decorated on most of their outward face. This is considerably more than any other passage-tomb anywhere in Ireland or Europe.

Second from left, a concrete slab indicates the position of a missing kerbstone

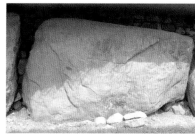

K 57

K 56

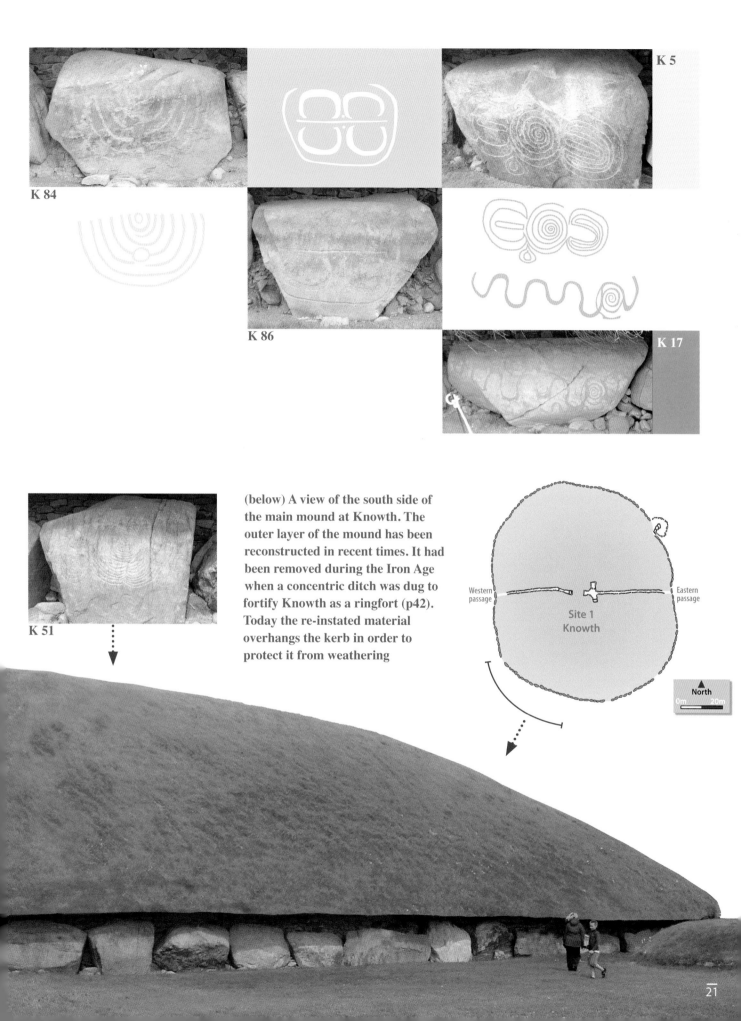

K 84

K 5

K 86

K 17

K 51

(below) A view of the south side of the main mound at Knowth. The outer layer of the mound has been reconstructed in recent times. It had been removed during the Iron Age when a concentric ditch was dug to fortify Knowth as a ringfort (p42). Today the re-instated material overhangs the kerb in order to protect it from weathering

Western passage

Eastern passage

Site 1
Knowth

North

0m   20m

Satellite Tombs

There are a large number of smaller satellite tombs clustered around the main mound of Knowth. These were built before or at the same time as the great mound itself. There are the remains of 17 satellite tombs with some evidence of a further three.

Some of the satellite tombs at Knowth are very large structures in themselves. Site 2 and 15 are the fifth and sixth largest passage-tombs in Brú na Bóinne. Site 2 is situated immediately to the south of the larger tomb and is 23 metres in diameter and contains a passage over 10 metres long. All the passages of the satellite tombs are orientated in the direction of the main mound or the entrance areas.

All of the satellite tombs were destroyed (during the Early Christian era) to the level of the ground stones, so that much of the kerb, passage and chamber have survived, but the cairn and roof were destroyed. Fortunately, at most of the sites, enough evidence has survived to be able to reconstruct the satellite tombs in modern times.

Site 16. The re-aligned entrance is to the left of the mound

Site 16

A small gap in the kerb occurs on the northern side of Knowth's great mound. The gap is there to accommodate a much smaller passage-tomb, Site 16 (above), which was built at an earlier time. The builders of the great tomb (Site 1) showed deference by choosing not to sweep aside the smaller tomb to complete the kerb. They also chose not to build the bigger tomb a few metres further to the southwest. This probably meant that all passage-tombs, big and small, old and new, were considered important to the people of Brú na Bóinne. It may also signify that the exact positioning of the great mound at Knowth was of considerable importance to the builders.

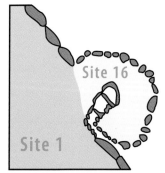

The builders of the bigger tomb also re-aligned the smaller tomb's passage. They built a right angle into the passage, the entrance of which is now running parallel with the kerb of the bigger tomb. Even after substantial modification and the building of a much larger tomb beside it, access to the chamber of Site 16 was still important.

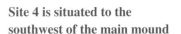
Site 4 is situated to the southwest of the main mound

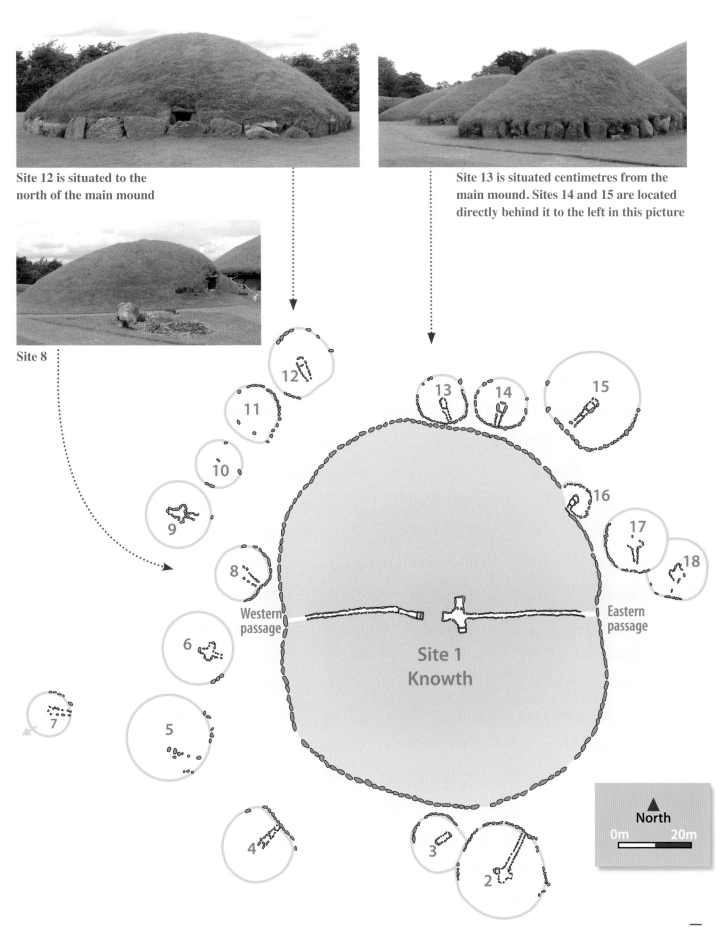

Site 12 is situated to the north of the main mound

Site 13 is situated centimetres from the main mound. Sites 14 and 15 are located directly behind it to the left in this picture

Site 8

12

11

10

9

8

Western passage

6

7

5

4

3

2

13

14

15

16

17

18

Eastern passage

Site 1
Knowth

North

0m   20m

Outside the entrances to the western and eastern tombs

The entrance stone of the western passage

The two entrance areas at Knowth contain many special features:

- A distinctively carved entrance stone. Both entrance stones are similar in design and display a vertical groove in the middle of the stone. Many of the best carved stones are located near the entrances.

- Special stones. A layer of quartz, rolled granite boulders and banded mudstone (below left) form a stone layer at ground level. At Newgrange this large quantity of quartz and granite boulders formed a wall in Neolithic times on the southern facade of the monument. This layer of stones at Knowth, it was decided at the time of the modern excavation, would remains in position on the ground, outside the entrances.

- Standing stones. There is one standing stone outside the eastern entrance and two outside the western entrance.

- Oval setting. These are stone-lined, saucer-shaped settings at ground level and are situated near the passage entrances. There are seven oval settings outside the eastern tomb and another six situated outside the western tomb entrance. Their diameter varies in size, the widest being 4 metres. Their purpose is unknown, but it is probable that they were associated with a grand ritual or ceremony at specific times of the year.

Kerbstone 15

Two standing stones mark the entrance to the western passage.

A similar vertical stone marks the entrance to the eastern passage

Kerbstone 15

This elaborately carved kerbstone is sometimes called the 'calendar' or 'sundial stone'.

Quartz, rolled granite boulders and mudstone

The white quartz was transported from the Wicklow Mountains 80km to the south. The rounded granite boulders were collected in Dundalk Bay c.50km to the north.

The entrance outside the eastern passage as it may have looked.

Many of the original features of the entrances have survived intact, despite centuries of disruption, including: all kerbstones, oval settings, standing stones and quartz layer.

Mound, tumulus, or cairn

Monument facade

All evidence of how the facade was originally constructed was lost when a deep ditch was cut inside the kerb during the Late Iron Age. It was decided at the time of the modern restoration not to reconstruct a stone facade. Today, grass forms the outer layer of the mound.

Possible roof-box

A roof-box structure similar to that found at Newgrange may have existed above the doorway at the eastern entrance. Its purpose would have been to allow sunlight at dawn on the autumn and vernal equinoxes to penetrate the passage and chamber of the eastern tomb of Knowth.

Door stone

A large flat stone, similar to the one found at Newgrange, may have existed to seal the tomb when not in use.

Entrance stone (Kerbstone 11)

Standing stone

Oval settings (7)

Scale: The standing stone is 1.6m high.

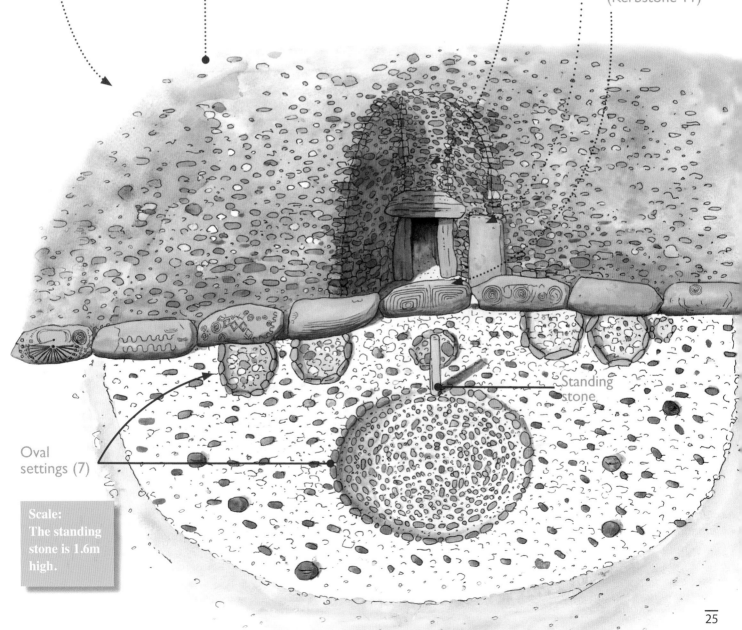

25

Inside Knowth

The great mound or tumulus of Knowth houses two of the great European megalithic interiors, surpassing most other megalithic structures in complexity, scale and decoration. The two passages at Knowth are roughly aligned east and west. The chambers which lie at the end of the passages remain intact and virtually unaltered, 5,000 years after they were built.

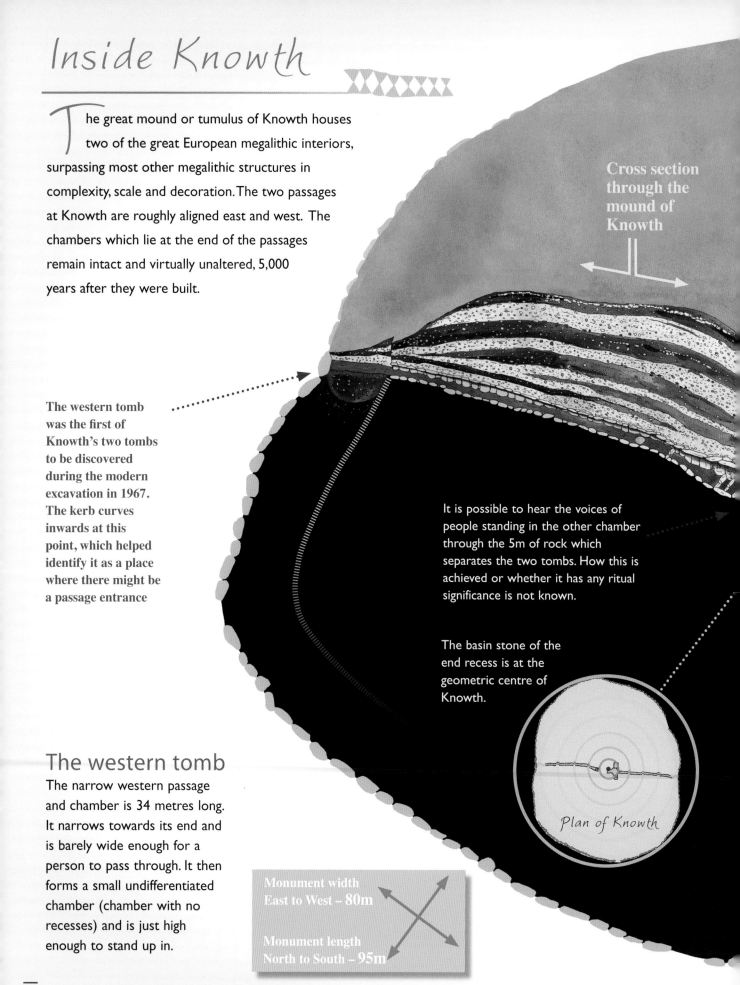

Cross section through the mound of Knowth

The western tomb was the first of Knowth's two tombs to be discovered during the modern excavation in 1967. The kerb curves inwards at this point, which helped identify it as a place where there might be a passage entrance

It is possible to hear the voices of people standing in the other chamber through the 5m of rock which separates the two tombs. How this is achieved or whether it has any ritual significance is not known.

The basin stone of the end recess is at the geometric centre of Knowth.

Plan of Knowth

The western tomb

The narrow western passage and chamber is 34 metres long. It narrows towards its end and is barely wide enough for a person to pass through. It then forms a small undifferentiated chamber (chamber with no recesses) and is just high enough to stand up in.

Monument width East to West – 80m

Monument length North to South – 95m

The chambers as tombs

A large amount of cremated bone and a small number of grave goods were found in the floor of both tombs during excavations in the modern era. Among the most common finds in passage-tombs are teeth, which often survive the cremation process intact.

The mound was constructed using alternating layers of stones, boulder clay and shale.

People living on and around Knowth in much later centuries, cut their own passages, called souterrains, through the mound (see p.45). They were used for storage and safety in times of attack.

**Satellite tomb
(Site 16)**

The eastern passage is orientated towards the rising sun on the morning of the equinox (March 21st and September 22nd), when the length of the day is as long as the night. The western passage is aligned to sunset on the same days.

Ditches cut into the mound behind the kerb during the Early Christian period, destroyed the original entrances to both passages for a distance of about 4 metres. This destruction means the sun's rays can no longer penetrate the passage of both tombs.

The long eastern passage

The eastern tomb

The eastern tomb consists of a passage and a cruciform chamber with three recesses. Its combined length is 40 metres.

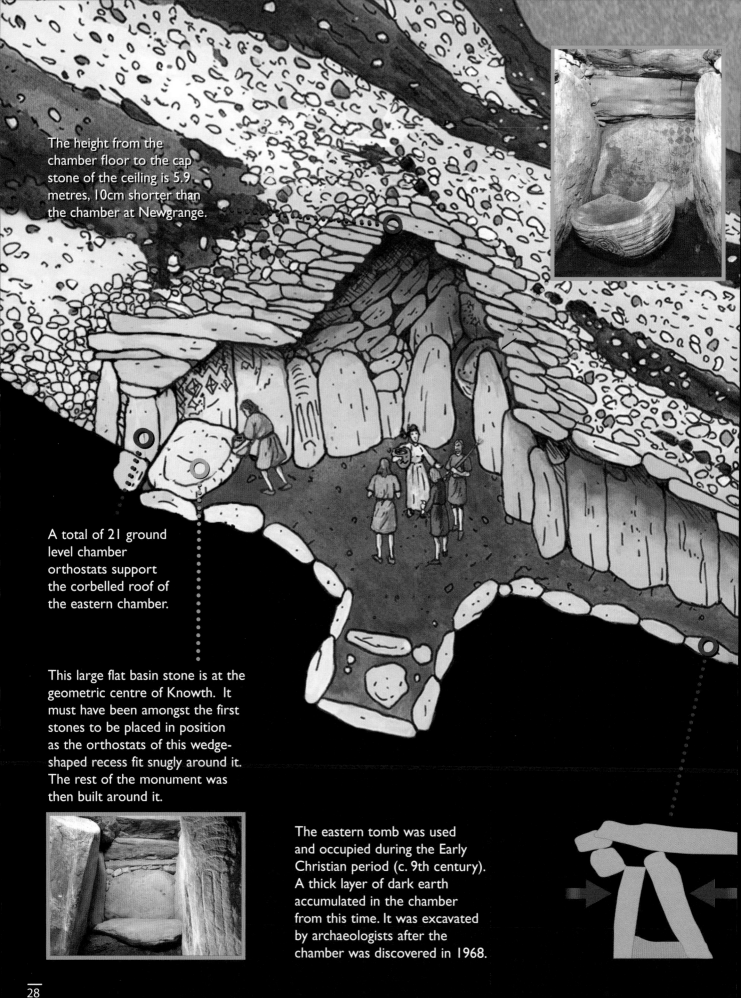

The height from the chamber floor to the cap stone of the ceiling is 5.9 metres, 10cm shorter than the chamber at Newgrange.

A total of 21 ground level chamber orthostats support the corbelled roof of the eastern chamber.

This large flat basin stone is at the geometric centre of Knowth. It must have been amongst the first stones to be placed in position as the orthostats of this wedge-shaped recess fit snugly around it. The rest of the monument was then built around it.

The eastern tomb was used and occupied during the Early Christian period (c. 9th century). A thick layer of dark earth accumulated in the chamber from this time. It was excavated by archaeologists after the chamber was discovered in 1968.

The eastern tomb

The eastern chamber at Knowth is one of the most impressive and intact structures from the Neolithic Age. Cruciform in plan, there are three smaller recesses, each containing a basin stone, which were used to hold the cremated remains of the dead.

The eastern chamber is one of the oldest multi-purpose rooms in the world. Its primary purpose is that of a tomb, but the large floor space and its high ceiling is clearly designed to accommodate people and we can only guess as to its role, religious or ceremonial, in Neolithic times. It is remarkably similar to the single chamber at nearby Newgrange.

From this point in the passage the roof begins to rise, reaching its apex in the centre of the chamber. The builders realised that the void that existed where the passageway meets the chamber was a weak point, which risked the collapse of the entire structure at some point in time. The solution was to begin the climb of the chamber roof much further down the passageway, thereby spreading the downward pressure, from above, over a greater area.

The great weight of the mound, over the centuries, has meant that some of the orthostats of the passage have fallen together. Today because of this, access to the eastern chamber is restricted and archaeologists and scholars have to crawl on all fours at various points to gain entry.

The basin stone (above) of the right recess of the eastern chamber is the most impressive of its type in Brú na Bóinne and Ireland. The stone was first carved into a bowl shape and its entire surface was then decorated with carving. It closely resembles a smaller 'stone urn' found near Knowth in 1725, which is now lost.

Two large vertical stones (below right) impede access to the right recess to just 50cm. The huge size and weight of the basin stone meant it would have been impossible to carry it up the eastern tomb's narrow passage. It, like the basin stone of the end recess, was probably placed in position at the commencement of building.

(left) The end recess of the eastern chamber from ground level to capstone. The horizontal wooden support beam is modern

Comparisons

The eastern chamber at Knowth bears a striking similarity to the single chamber of its near neighbour, Newgrange (in plan on right).

Both have:

- cruciform chambers with three smaller recesses

- long passages, though the eastern passage and chamber at Knowth (40m) is much longer than that at Newgrange (24m)

- curves incorporated into their passages. At Newgrange the curves serve to reduce the amount of indirect sunlight entering the chamber.

It seems likely, given the proximity and the similarity of design of Knowth and Newgrange, that they were built within a short time of each other. To build one chamber of such complexity was a towering achievement. To repeat the process reaffirms the incredible skill and ambition of the builders of Brú na Bóinne.

Neither chamber is truly symmetrical, both chambers follow the same deviations, the right recess being slightly higher than the left recess.

The right recess is the largest recess and is semi-enclosed. It also houses the most elaborate basin stone.

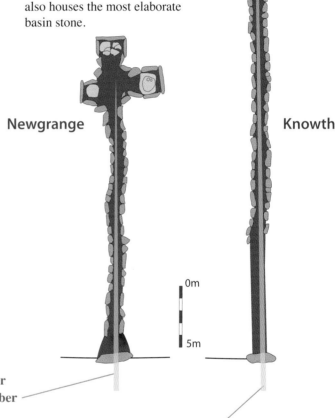

Newgrange   Knowth

0m

5m

The three great monuments of Brú na Bóinne – Knowth, Dowth and Newgrange – in plan, comparing orientation and scale of the passages and chambers

Path of sunlight at sunrise on the winter solstice, 21st December

Possible path of sunlight around the time of the spring (22th March) and autumn equinox (22nd September) at sunrise.

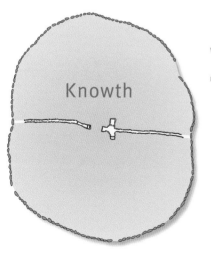

Knowth

N
W E
S

10m

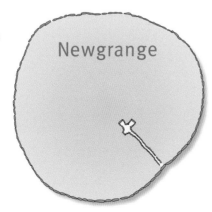

Newgrange

Dowth

In the early eighth century when people were living on the mound of Knowth, this and other inscriptions were cut into the western passage. Some are in the early Irish alphabet of ogham and others like this intruder's name, 'Teimtennac', are in an Irish 'Insular' script similar to the Book of Kells. Literacy was very rare at the time and was practiced mostly by the clergy and nobility. There are 20 Early Christian names carved into both tombs at Knowth, making it the largest hoard of historical graffiti in Ireland.

The western tomb

The western tomb at Knowth is the second longest passage and chamber in Europe, at 34 metres from the entrance of the passage to the rear of the chamber. The passage roof is at some points very low, barely one metre at its lowest. It gradually increases in height, so that visitors can stand only when they have reached the chamber (1.3 metres wide and 2 metres in height).

It is an undifferentiated tomb with no recesses, a style which is found in 10 of the satellite tombs at Knowth. Although it is much less impressive than its corbell-roofed companion the eastern tomb, its roof bears considerably more weight from the mound above. The western chamber's interior has survived unaltered with the weight of ten metres of stone above it, for five millennia.

The chambers smaller scale probably meant that there was much less ceremony associated with it and that it functioned primarily as a burial place.

There is a slight change of direction of 22° at this point

The only basin stone of the western tomb lies in the passage. It was probably originally located in the hollow before the second sill in the chamber. At some time in the last 5,000 years, unwelcome visitors (below) tried to steal the stone, but gave up and discarded it here

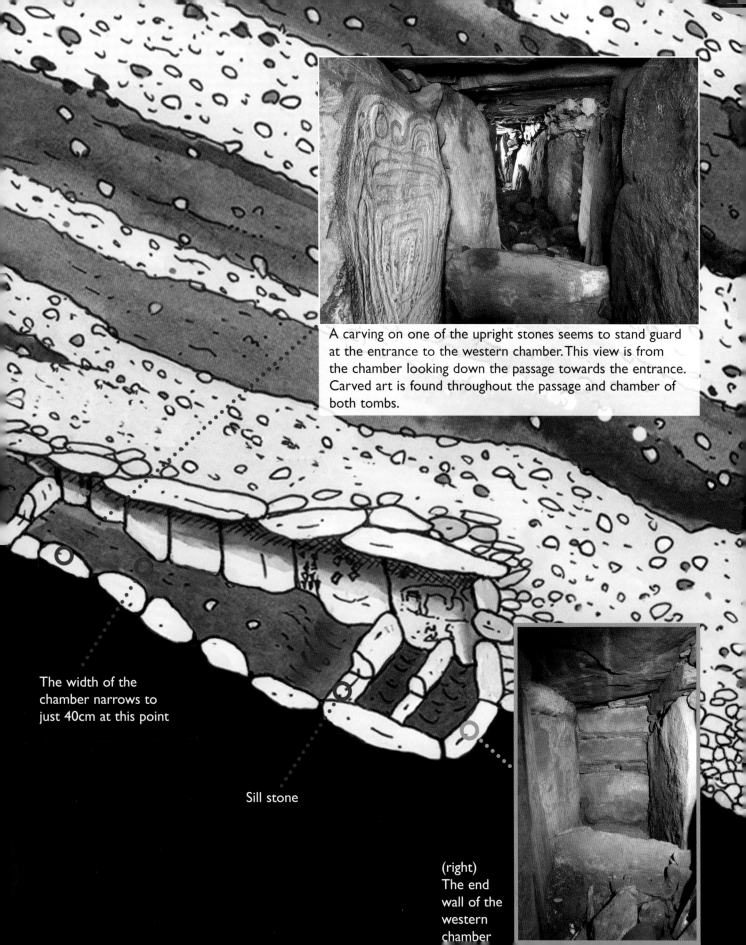

A carving on one of the upright stones seems to stand guard at the entrance to the western chamber. This view is from the chamber looking down the passage towards the entrance. Carved art is found throughout the passage and chamber of both tombs.

The width of the chamber narrows to just 40cm at this point

Sill stone

(right) The end wall of the western chamber

Cremation and burial rites

The burial rite at Brú na Bóinne was predominantly cremation during the Neolithic period. Despite disruption to the chambers of both tombs at Knowth throughout the centuries, enough cremated material has survived to establish that the number of burials was large, successive and over many generations. The cremated remains of over a hundred individuals have been identified in the right recess of the eastern chamber alone, half of whom were juveniles.

It is possible to speculate at Knowth that:

▌ the layout and features at the entrance to the passages indicate that there were elaborate ceremonies associated with the burial of the dead, probably at specific times of the year

▌ all members of the community were interred there. A lack of significant grave goods, apart from the macehead (p. 38), allows us to speculate that Knowth was the burial place of the wider community rather than just a social elite

▌ burial of the dead was centred around a belief in an afterlife. The passage-tombs of Brú na Bóinne formed a complex of buildings where the dead of the community could be reborn or united with their god or gods.

Burial goods are a feature of passage-tombs all over Europe and the excavation of both tombs at Knowth produced items such as bone pins, beads, pendants, balls of chalk and pottery. Some of these goods had been burned, indicating they were with the body of the deceased when they were cremated.

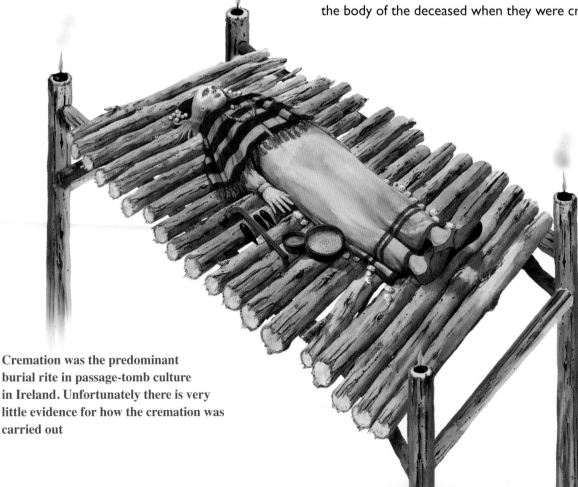

Cremation was the predominant burial rite in passage-tomb culture in Ireland. Unfortunately there is very little evidence for how the cremation was carried out

A family group gathers to place the cremated remains of a loved one on the basin stone in the left recess of the eastern chamber. All ages and sexes have been found interred in passage-tombs in Ireland.

The Art of Knowth

The stone carved art of Brú na Bóinne is the greatest concentration of megalithic art in Europe. Thirty per cent of all European megalithic art is found there, while Knowth accounts for nearly a half of the art of Brú na Bóinne. Not only is the carved art abundant, but its quality and sophistication has few equals anywhere. Of the Atlantic passage-tomb building regions, only Brittany (especially the tomb of Gavrinis) has carved art that can be compared stylistically to the art of Brú na Bóinne.

Tools made of flint, the hardest material of the stone age, were used to carve or pick designs in relief on the great sandstone megaliths of Knowth, as no metal tools yet existed. The proliferation of art at Newgrange, Dowth and especially Knowth proves that, despite the exhausting commitment to construction, art always formed an essential element of each of the monuments.

The position of art at Knowth

The positioning of art on over 250 stones at Knowth seems to have been deliberate and well thought out. Art is found:

- as free-standing objects such as basin stones, maceheads, and phallus objects (right)
- in the interior of the tombs, especially on the first level of vertical orthostats (below)
- on 90 of the 127 kerbstones.

(right)

There are over 11 different motifs used in the art of Brú na Bóinne. They are used alone and in conjunction with other motifs to form a bewildering array of patterns. The motifs fall into two groups, curvilinear (circles, spirals and radials) and rectilinear (parallel lines, chevrons and zigzags).

Interpretations of these carvings remain a mystery to us today. Prof Michael O'Kelly, excavator of Newgrange, explained, "that the motifs were probably symbolic, religious, or magical in context . . . and it is unlikely that we will ever discover what any of them meant since we cannot know the minds or the emotions of a people who did not know how to write and who are separated from us by more than 4,000 years".

There are many theories about the meaning of the art of Brú na Bóinne and each generation throws up new ideas, each one as relevant as the next.

There is no colour pigment on the carved stones of Knowth, though colour has been found on passage-tomb carvings in the Iberian peninsula as well as habitation sites in the Orkney Islands

The Knowth Macehead

T he macehead (right) was found in the right hand recess of the eastern chamber of Knowth during excavations in 1982. It is one of the most extraordinary pieces of carving from the Neolithic world. A macehead is a ceremonial hammer head and is usually connected to a wooden shaft.

The flint stone with which the macehead was made originated in the Orkney Islands, just off the north coast of Scotland, an area rich in Neolithic monuments. Where the Knowth macehead was carved is not known, but the motifs on its six surfaces are typically found in the art of Brú na Bóinne.

The Knowth macehead is unmistakably the face of a man, making it the only carving from Brú na Bóinne that can be said to be truly representational. A beard, hair, eyes and a gaping mouth are created from simple geometric shapes. As such, it is the earliest representation of a face in Irish art and perhaps the earliest representation of an actual Irish person or deity.

Today, the macehead can be seen in the archaeology section of the National Museum of Ireland on Dublin's Kildare Street along with other artefacts found at Knowth and Brú na Bóinne.

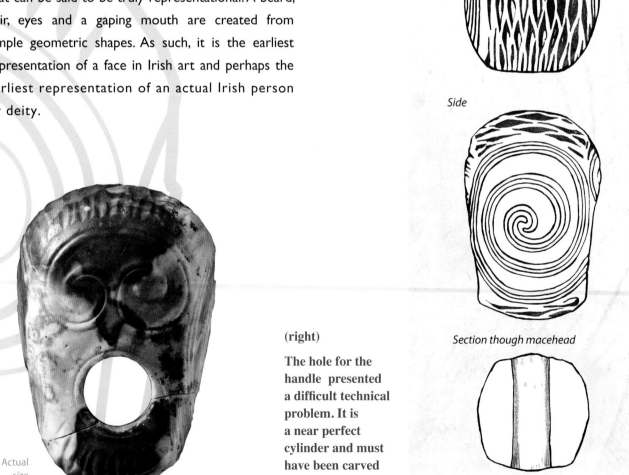

Top

Side

Section though macehead

Actual size

(right)

The hole for the handle presented a difficult technical problem. It is a near perfect cylinder and must have been carved using a bow drill

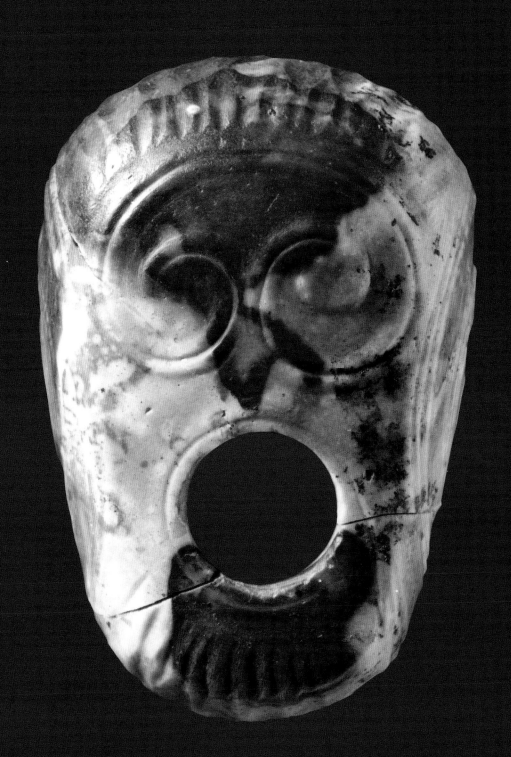

Knowth through the ages

As well as being a place of religious and social importance in the Neolithic Age, the great mound of Knowth was for many centuries a home and a place of refuge and defence. The modern excavation at Knowth has revealed layer upon layer of human activity for over 5,000 years. Knowth is a microcosm of Irish archaeology, with most of the main phases of cultural development in Ireland represented. There are few archaeological sites in the world that have seen so many different uses, over such a long period of time.

**Neolithic Knowth
c. 3000BC**

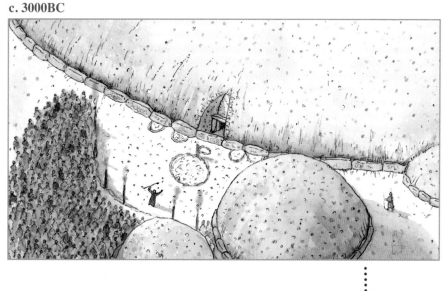

**(far right)
A modern reconstruction of the wood henge monument which is situated close to the entrance of the eastern passage**

	4000BC		3000BC		2000BC
Brú na Bóinne ➡			The great tombs of Knowth, Dowth and Newgrange are built c.3300 – 2900BC	A new culture known as 'Grooved ware' people build small wood henge monument at Knowth	'Beaker' people live around Knowth. They use satellite tomb (no.15) for a burial
Ireland ➡	Middle Stone Age people (hunter gatherers) in Ireland	First farmers in Ireland / Carrowmore Megalithic Cemetery, Co Sligo. It is amongst the earliest in Europe		First metal production in Ireland	

Mesolithic (Middle Stone Age)   Neolithic (New Stone Age)   Bronze Age

World ➡	The wheel is invented in the Middle East	Great Pyramid (Cheops) of Giza c.2560BC	Sarcen phase of Stonehenge c.2500BC	Moses leads Hebrews out of Egypt c.1400BC

←   **P r e h i s t o r i c   e r a   i n   I r e l a n d**   →

The first known use of the land at Knowth was revealed when excavations discovered the post holes of a palisaded Neolithic house which ran under the mound of Knowth. It was therefore built before the monument, circa 3500BC, about 500 years before the great passage-tomb was completed. At some point the house was abandoned and in the following centuries the passage-tomb builders began their work on the earlier satellite tombs and then the great mound itself.

Very little is known about where the passage-tomb builders themselves lived and there is evidence for only a small number of houses of this period in the area.

The Bronze Age

A new culture, known today as 'Grooved ware' people (from their pottery) eventually replaced the original builders of Knowth and Brú na Bóinne. By this time (2500BC) the passage-tombs of Knowth had ceased to be used for burials and were falling into disrepair. It is clear that they believed Knowth to be a sacred site, as a small wooden henge monument was built close to the entrance of the eastern tomb.

Another culture, 'Beaker' people (known for their distinctive shaped pottery) chose to live around the site in about 2300BC during the Bronze Age. They used a satellite tomb (site 15) to bury one of their dead and left one of their pots as a grave good. Beaker people lived around Knowth for about 200 years and then abandoned the site.

Knowth lay dormant for the next 2,000 years, known probably in local mythology, as the tomb of gods or ancient ancestors.

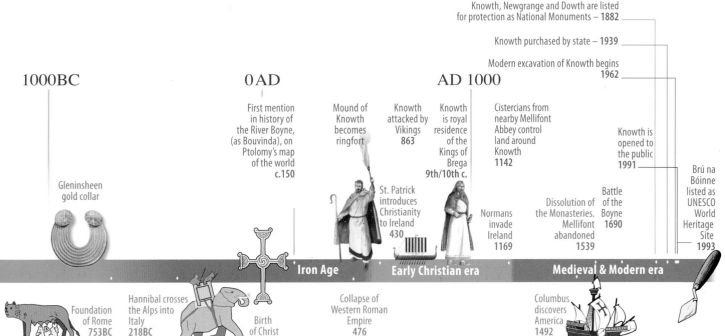

Knowth, Newgrange and Dowth are listed for protection as National Monuments – **1882**

Knowth purchased by state – **1939**

Modern excavation of Knowth begins **1962**

1000BC

0 AD

AD 1000

First mention in history of the River Boyne, (as Bouvinda), on Ptolomy's map of the world c.150

Mound of Knowth becomes ringfort

Knowth attacked by Vikings **863**

Knowth is royal residence of the Kings of Brega 9th/10th c.

Cistercians from nearby Mellifont Abbey control land around Knowth **1142**

Knowth is opened to the public **1991**

Brú na Bóinne listed as UNESCO World Heritage Site **1993**

Gleninsheen gold collar

St. Patrick introduces Christianity to Ireland **430**

Normans invade Ireland **1169**

Dissolution of the Monasteries. Mellifont abandoned **1539**

Battle of the Boyne **1690**

Iron Age

Early Christian era

Medieval & Modern era

Foundation of Rome **753BC**

Hannibal crosses the Alps into Italy **218BC**

Birth of Christ

Collapse of Western Roman Empire **476**

Columbus discovers America **1492**

Historic era in Ireland

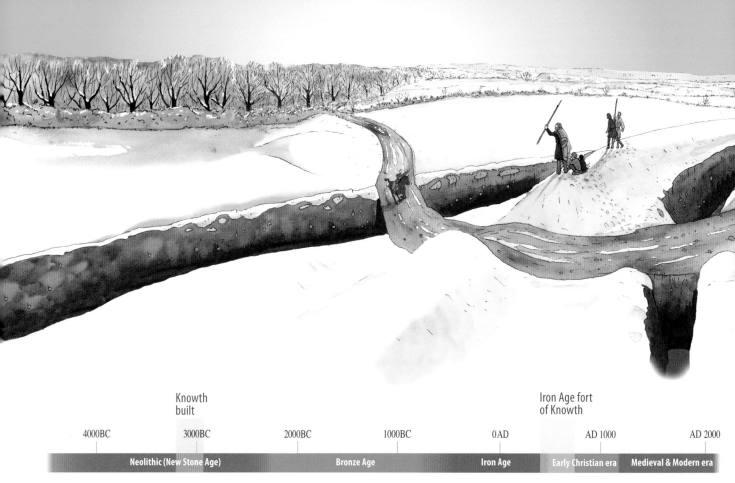

Knowth
built

Iron Age fort
of Knowth

4000BC	3000BC	2000BC	1000BC	0AD	AD 1000	AD 2000

Neolithic (New Stone Age)	Bronze Age	Iron Age	Early Christian era	Medieval & Modern era

The Late Iron Age

In the Late Iron Age, people once again chose the mound of Knowth as a place to live. It proved to be an ideal defensive position in turbulent times, with a view for many kilometres across the surrounding countryside. Knowth is also positioned just above the River Boyne and was an ideal place to control commercial traffic on its way to and from central Ireland. Two concentric circular ditches were dug to enhance a ready-made 'ring fort', destroying the entrances to both Neolithic passageways in the process.

Thirty burials found in and around Knowth during the modern excavation date to just before the Late Iron Age occupation, including a double burial of two young men (right). Both were decapitated and were buried head to toe. A set of gaming dice made of bone and some counters were buried with them.

For a short time and for reasons unknown, Knowth was abandoned in the early eighth century.

(above and left)
**Late Iron/Early Christian era Knowth,
5th – 8th centuries AD**

The Early Christian period

In the Early Christian period (c. 800AD), Knowth became a home again, this time for the kings of North Brega, who made it their royal residence. The territory of North Brega encompassed all the land from the River Liffey to Armagh. In 944 it was the seat (capital) of Congallach Cnobha (Congallach of Knowth) who was high king of Ireland for over a decade.

A great deal of metal working material was found from this period during the modern excavation, including bronze and gold, which testifies to Knowth as a major centre of art, industry and wealth. This was a 'golden age' of Irish art, when artefacts such as the Ardagh chalice and Tara brooch (found 15km away) were produced in Irish workshops.

It was at this time that literature, newly arrived in Ireland, began to mention Brú na Bóinne as a place of importance. It is clear from these texts that those living on the mound of Knowth and in Brú na Bóinne were aware of its association with other past ancient cultures. It was believed by the Early Christians that Brú na Bóinne was

4000BC	3000BC	2000BC	1000BC	0AD	AD 1000	AD 2000
	Knowth built				Knowth, capital of North Brega	

Neolithic (New Stone Age) — Bronze Age — Iron Age — Early Christian era — Medieval & Modern era

Early Christian Knowth, 8th – 12th centuries AD

the place where the Tuatha Dé Danann (thought to be the first inhabitants of Ireland) went underground, when the Gaelic Irish arrived in Ireland. It is surprising then, that these early historic people should choose to live in such close proximity to what they may have considered to be the entrance to the underworld.

Several other large ringforts were built in Brú na Bóinne in this period, including a very large one (right), which survives today only 400 metres south of Knowth.

Early Christian souterrains

Souterrain – from French 'sous terrain', meaning underground

Nine souterrains were constructed at Knowth at some time in the 9th or 10th century AD, one of the largest concentrations anywhere in Ireland. They are stone lined, underground chambers, accessed by a narrow passage, the entrance to which was usually hidden. Souterrains are common in the Irish countryside and are often associated with ringforts.

They were often used for storage, as they were dry and maintained a constant temperature of 10° Celsius. Their main purpose however, was to provide a safe place to retreat to, if the primary defences of the ringfort failed, in the event of attack.

In many cases the souterrain had a built-in trap, which made it easy for those sheltering inside to defend the inner chamber (below). Invaders were forced to wriggle uncomfortably through a tight gap and could be attacked by defenders who were in a better position to wield weapons.

Unfortunately the souterrain defences at Knowth did fail. We know from contemporary literature that 'the caves' of Knowth and Dowth were looted. A large fleet of Norse (Vikings) ships sailed up the Boyne and attacked the royal residence of Knowth on at least three occasions. It is clear from the same sources that the people of Knowth in alliance with other kingdoms, gave as good as they got, attacking Viking Dublin on several occasions.

The large number of souterrains at Knowth, may have had an altogether more sinister purpose. Archaeological evidence indicates that some of the souterrain doors open only from the outside, prompting the theory that they were used to keep the most valuable commodity of the time, the slave, tightly locked away.

The Norman period

The Cistercians founded their first monastery in Ireland at Mellifont in 1142, not far from Brú na Bóinne, and took possession of all the surrounding land. They named the lands within Brú na Bóinne, 'New Grange' (a grange is an outlying farm). They brought religious, agricultural and architectural influences from France to the region.

In the late 12th century the Normans arrived in Ireland intent on military conquest. Part of their strategy for long term domination of the country was the building of castles at important points. To this end they built their own fortress on the mound at Knowth, the foundations of which were revealed during the modern excavation.

By the middle of the 14th century the fort at Knowth had been abandoned, possibly because of the black death, which ravaged Ireland and Europe in 1348. In 1539 Henry VIII, as part of the Reformation, dissolved the monasteries of Ireland and the Cistercian influence at Brú na Bóinne waned.

The Battle of the Boyne

On 12th July 1690 the sleepy fields around Knowth awoke to become a battlefield on a European scale. The Battle of the Boyne was fought between the two rival claimants to the English, Scottish and Irish thrones – the Catholic King James and the Protestant King William – drawing in forces from all over Europe. Both kings were present and in command of their troops.

A stalemate was ensuing with William's force unable to cross from the north side of the river to attack James on the south side at Oldbridge, at the eastern end of Brú na Bóinne. William sent a force of nearly 9,000 men (a quarter of his army) to ford the Boyne at Rosnaree, just below Knowth. It proved to be the most decisive engagement of the battle. James believed it to be a significant move against his position and moved half his army to oppose it. William, with most of his army still in position at Oldbridge, was then able to cross the river. James's depleted force was forced to retire from the battlefield in defeat.

King James, with much of his force deserting, fled Ireland and went into exile in France, where he died in 1701.

Cistercian (Norman) Knowth, late 12th–early 14th century AD

| | | Knowth built | | | | | | Norman Knowth | Modern Knowth |
| 4000BC | | 3000BC | | 2000BC | | 1000BC | | 0AD | | AD 1000 | | AD 2000 |

| Neolithic (New Stone Age) | Bronze Age | Iron Age | Early Christian era | Medieval & Modern era |

Modern times

The 19th and 20th centuries witnessed a growing interest in the past by scholars and the general public alike. The many abandoned castles, earth works and monuments which covered the Irish countryside were now looked at in a new light by the first professional historians and archaeologists.

Scientific investigation at Knowth began in the late 19th century, culminating in the modern archaeological excavation of the late 20th century. It revealed Knowth to be every bit as interesting as its famous neighbour, Newgrange and the greatest building of the European Neolithic Age.

With a large amount of the site excavated, the work of conservation began: the re-alignment of some of the passage orthostats, the rebuilding of some of the satellite tombs and the sheltering of the kerbstones from the worst of the weather. Visitor facilities were

also installed at Knowth as part of the wider access to Brú na Bóinne, all of which tell the story of the monument and its subsequent history over the five millennia since it was built. The visitor facilities were also designed to protect the monument for future generations to appreciate.

Public interest in Knowth has continued to grow with every revelation and discovery. In 1991 Knowth was opened to the public and two years later Brú na Bóinne was listed as a UNESCO World Heritage site.

The work of investigation at Knowth, begun in the 19th century and continued into the modern era is far from over. Every generation brings forth a new discovery or theory, which challenges long held beliefs about the largest and most complex building of the Irish Neolithic, the people that built it and their desire to mark forever, in stone, the landscape of Brú na Bóinne.

Knowth looking east. The narrow entrance to the western tomb is visible in the near side of the main mound